The Shots Book

A Little Brother's Superhero Tale

by

Ethan Posard

ABOUT ETHAN

My big sister is a student filmmaker who wrote the documentary, Invisible Threat; a peer-to-peer film that explores the science of vaccines and outbreaks.

While she was making the film I was due to get a shot for school and she wanted to document my experience. My parents said I needed the shot to prevent me from getting sick but that didn't convince me.

However, after I learned about herd immunity and saw first hand what happens to the vulnerable when it breaks down, I gladly got my shot. It was surprising to me that kids aren't taught about community immunity and it wasn't in our school science textbooks.

This inspired me to write a children's illustrated book about what I learned about shots, protecting my health, and the health of babies in my community. It is everything I wish I had known when I was getting my kindergarden shots in a story about how my puppy and I became community immunity superheroes, but based on my real life experience.

This book is dedicated to children who rely on herd immunity to keep them safe. When you buy my book another book gets donated to a Children's Hospital Library. Kids fighting cancer, needing transplants, or battling other diseases are the real heroes and I want them to know they have a friend who cares. I'm 14 and #IAmTheHerd.

My name is Ethan and I'm a kid just like you. This is a true story of what I learned about protecting my health and the health of babies in my community. This is also a story about how my puppy and I became community immunity superheroes.

My adventure started when my parents told me I needed to get a shot, also called a vaccine, for school. My big sister took that as an opportunity to ask me lots of questions for a movie she was making about shots.

Sometimes being a little brother is challenging.

My parents said I needed the vaccine to keep me from getting sick. Being healthy is important, but why can't I just do all the other things to keep me healthy and skip the shot?

Eating healthy foods like fruits and vegetables helps keep me healthy.

Drinking water instead of sugary drinks helps keep me healthy.

Frequently washing my hands with soap and water, especially before I eat, helps keep me healthy.

Getting lots of exercise and going to bed at my bedtime helps keep me healthy.

Always covering my sneezes or coughs into my arm keeps me from spreading germs, and that helps keep others healthy.

So if we all do these important things to keep us healthy, why do I still need to get a shot?

Then my puppy, Roxy, suddenly got very very sick and I got the answer to my question.

We did everything to keep Roxy healthy. We gave her the healthiest puppy food, puppy vitamins, and a pampered puppy home, but she still got very sick, and that was very scary.

Her doctor said Roxy might have a terrible disease that could have been prevented by a vaccine. This is called a vaccine preventable disease. Scientists created vaccines to keep puppies (and children) from getting some very serious illnesses caused by very bad germs.

The only way to protect little puppies is for older dogs to get all their vaccines, making a shield so illnesses can't get into our community and spread. This is called herd immunity.

A vaccine has a special medicine that helps the body make a protective shield so that those germs can't get them sick. However, a puppy has to be old enough and healthy enough to get the shot.

Roxy was too young to get the vaccine.

Animals like elephants protect their babies by circling the herd around the vulnerable. The herd works together to create a shield around the baby elephant to protect them. Herd immunity only works if everyone does their part.

When everyone works together some awful diseases can be wiped out completely. Smallpox was defeated with vaccines and we no longer need to get that shot. Hopefully soon polio will also be defeated and we won't need that vaccine either.

It didn't seem fair for little puppies too young to get their vaccines, like Roxy, to get sick from diseases that are preventable.

Roxy got better and as soon as she was old enough, she got all her vaccines. She could now go on walks and to the dog park. Roxy was also protecting other little puppies from getting sick through herd immunity. Roxy deserved a doggie super hero cape.

Just like Roxy, after we get our vaccines we get a protective force field that keeps us from getting sick and from getting babies sick.

There are also many kids who aren't lucky enough to get shots. Kids who have cancer or other illnesses can't get vaccines. They need us to protect them through herd immunity too.

Now that's a great superpower.

After learning this of course I wanted to do my part to protect babies and sick kids, while also protecting my own health. I was ready to be a community immunity superhero and even let my big sister film me getting my vaccine.

I think all kids should be celebrated and get superhero capes when we get our vaccines. We are protecting our community and should be proud to share that.

Herd immunity protection was especially important for my family, because my aunt was *very* pregnant with twins.

When my tiny cousins were born I was so proud that I had my protective super power to help keep Katie and Lauren safe. I would have felt terrible if I got them or any other baby sick.

The worst part of getting a shot is worrying about it, so instead start superhero training.

Pick a treat with your parents to celebrate becoming a superhero. Make a fun list and be very brave--maybe you'll get two treats.

Remember, millions of kids just like you are getting their vaccinations because their parents want to protect them and their community. So be tough, be brave, be proud, and say it loud with us, "I am the herd!"

Ethan & Roxy's Superhero Tips:

Make a superhero pal. Get a favorite stuffed animal, give him a cape, and bring them to your doctor's appointment.

Don't look at the shot, look at your superhero pal.

Try to relax and tell your superhero pal who you want to protect in your community.

When it's time for your shot, blow on your superhero's cape so it flutters.

Afterwards, take a picture showing off your bandage while making a muscle pose and share it.

If you'd like to share your photo with Roxy and me, have your parents use the hashtag #IAmTheHerd in the picture and send it to us via TheShotsBook.com